100 MIND-BLOWING SOCCER FACTS

100 Unbelievable Stories That Prove Soccer is the Craziest Sport

FELIX GRAYSON

Copyright © 2025 by MindSpark Publishing

All rights reserved. No part of this book may be reproduced, stored in a retrieval system, or transmitted in any form or by any means—electronic, mechanical, photocopying, recording, or otherwise—without the prior written permission of the publisher, except in the case of brief quotations embodied in critical articles or reviews.

This book is intended to provide general information on the topics discussed and is not intended as a substitute for professional advice. Every effort has been made to ensure accuracy, but the author and publisher assume no responsibility for errors, omissions, or contrary interpretation of the subject matter.

Published by MindSpark Publishing.
Cover design by MindSpark Publishing.

CONTENTS

Before We Dive In... 8
Introduction 10
The Game That Lasted Three Days 13
The Day a Dog Won Man of the Match 15
The Referee Who Pulled Out a White Card 17
The Game That Was Played on Two Continents 19
The Match That Had No Ball 21
The Goalkeeper Who Scored More Goals Than Most Strikers 23
The World Cup That Was Stolen 25
The Player Who Got a Red Card Before the Game Even Started 27
The Match That Was Delayed by a Swarm of Bees 29
The Fastest Red Card in History 31
The Goal That Was Scored in Just 2 Seconds 33
The Referee Who Booked Himself 35
The Game That Ended 149-0 37
The Fan Who Got Signed After One Kick 39
The Player Who Was Sold for 100 Kilograms of Meat 41
The Soccer Ball That Saved a Man's Life 43
The Soccer Team That Was Banned for Winning Too Much 45
The Match That Was Played Without a Ball 47
The Goal That Was Scored by the Wind 49
The Time a Player Bit a Chunk Off Another Player's Ear ... 51
The Game That Was Played at 16,000 Feet 53

The Time a Goalkeeper Scored from His Own Box 55

The Match That Was Played With Only 7 Players 57

The Player Who Wore Five Different Jerseys in One Match 59

The Player Who Was Sent Off Three Times in One Game 61

The Goalkeeper Who Wore a Cap for Superstition 63

The Referee Who Brought a Gun Onto the Field 65

The World Cup That Was Won by a Coin Toss 67

The Time a Player Disguised Himself as a Teammate 69

The Match That Was Stopped by a Parrot 71

The Player Who Missed a Game Because of a Video Game 73

The Goal That Was Scored by a Toilet Paper Roll 75

The Player Who Brought His Own Penalty Spot 77

The Team That Scored Without Touching the Ball 79

The Time a Team Won a Game with Just One Shot 81

The Coach Who Got Himself Sent Off on Purpose 83

The Time a Goalkeeper Used a Water Bottle to Save a Penalty 85

The Match That Had 22 Red Cards 87

Goal Disallowed by a Fan's Whistle 89

The Player Who Scored a Hat-Trick in Just 70 Seconds 91

The Match That Was Played in Three Different Days 93

The Time a Goalkeeper Was Sent Off After 10 Seconds 95

The Player Who Scored Five Own Goals in One Game 97

The Time a Goal Was Scored from a Throw-In… Almost 99

The Player Who Brought a Chicken Onto the Field 101

The Match That Was Stopped Because of Too Many Balloons 103

The Player Who Wore Two Different Shoes in a Match 105

The Time a Goal Was Scored After Just 2 Touches 107

The Team That Forgot to Bring Their Jerseys 109

The Game That Was Played in a Prison 111

The Time a Goalkeeper Played With a Broken Arm 113

The Player Who Was Signed Because of a Video Game 115

The Time a Team Celebrated Too Early and Lost 117

Referee Used Rock, Paper, Scissors to Decide a Match 119

The Player Who Scored While Tying His Shoelaces 121

The Time a Player Got a Red Card for Kissing the Referee 123

The Game That Had Three Halves 125

The Time a Streaker Scored a Goal 127

The Player Who Scored a Goal While Lying Down 129

The Referee Who Used a Spray Can to Draw a Line 131

The Match That Was Played With a Square Ball 133

The Time a Goalkeeper Scored with His Backside 135

The Player Who Was Substituted After Just 1 Second 137

The Soccer Game That Was Played Underwater 139

The Player Who Scored While Taking a Drink 141

The Time a Referee Gave a Penalty Kick by Accident 143

The Team That Won a Game Without Taking a Single Shot 145

The Goalkeeper Who Took a Nap During a Match 147

The Player Who Scored With His Face 149

The Game That Was Stopped Because of Too Much Fog 151

The Player Who Got a Yellow Card for Celebrating Too Much 153

The Player Who Brought His Dog Onto the Field 155

The Time a Player Got a Red Card for Winking 157

The Time a Fan Snuck Onto the Field and Played 159

The Goalkeeper Who Wore the Number 10 Jersey 161

The Player Who Wore a Wig During a Match 163

The Match That Was Delayed Because of a Sheep 165

The Goalkeeper Who Used a Towel for Good Luck 167

The Time a Team Walked Off Because of a Bad Smell 169

The Time a Dog Saved a Goal 171

The Player Who Got a Red Card for Kicking a Balloon 173

The Game That Was Played on a Floating Pitch 175

The Time a Fan Controlled the Stadium Sprinklers 177

The Time a Player Got a Yellow Card for Farting 179

The Goal That Was Disallowed Because of a Fan's Whistle 181

The Time a Referee Forgot His Cards 183

The Player Who Got Sent Off for Celebrating With the Fans 185

The Time a Ball Burst Mid-Air 187

The Player Who Changed His Name to Avoid a Curse 189

The Time a Goalkeeper Scored Without Kicking the Ball 191

The Player Who Brought a Selfie Stick Onto the Field 193

The Player Who Was Sent Off for Tackling a Teammate 195

The Match That Was Stopped by a Drone 197

The Time a Referee Used a Red Card on a Coach's Chair 199

The Player Who Got a Yellow Card for Imitating the Referee 201

The Match That Was Stopped Because of Too Many Red Cards ... 203

The Player Who Was Substituted Before Kickoff 205

Goalkeeper Scored With His Head in the Last Second 207

The Player Who Scored a Goal While Tying His Shorts 209

The Game That Lasted Only 2 Seconds 211
Conclusion 212
Acknowledgements 214
About the Author 216

BEFORE WE DIVE IN...

Did you know that this is just **one** of many **mind-blowing** books waiting to be discovered?

What if I told you there's a **world of jaw-dropping, unbelievable, and downright bizarre facts** across **sports, science, history, mysteries, and more**—each one packed with stories that will **challenge what you thought you knew?**

EVER WONDERED WHAT IT'S LIKE TO...

- Witness **record-breaking Olympic moments** that defy human limits?

- Explore **real-life conspiracy theories** that sound too wild to be true?

- Discover **unsolved mysteries** that still leave experts baffled?

- Learn about **billionaires, stock market**

crashes, and money secrets?

- Find out how **robots, AI, and space travel** are shaping the future?

- Experience the **most extreme sports, legendary battles, and shocking events?**

This is just the beginning. The **100 Mind-Blowing series** covers it **all.**

WANT TO SEE WHAT'S NEXT?

Go to **FelixGrayson.com** and explore the **growing collection** of books and audiobooks that will **entertain, amaze, and keep you coming back for more.**

Curiosity doesn't stop here—this is just the beginning. What will blow your mind next?

INTRODUCTION

Welcome to *100 Mind-Blowing Soccer Facts*, a collection designed to make you say, **"Wait, that actually happened?"** From bizarre goals to wild rulebook loopholes, this book is packed with **unbelievable stories** that will make you look at the beautiful game in a whole new way.

Have you ever heard about the time a **dog saved a goal**, or when a referee **gave a red card to a chair**? What about the match that was **stopped by a drone**, or the time a goalkeeper **scored with his backside**? These are just a few of the jaw-dropping moments waiting for you inside. Each story has been carefully chosen to **surprise, entertain, and leave you in absolute disbelief.**

Whether you're a lifelong soccer fanatic, a casual fan, or just someone who loves **crazy-but-true sports stories**, this book has something for everyone. Read it **cover to cover** or flip to a random page and see what catches your eye. No matter how you dive in, you're in for a **fun, fast-paced, and unforgettable ride** through soccer's strangest and most shocking moments.

So grab your favorite snack, find a cozy spot, and get ready to explore the **craziest, most mind-blowing stories** from the world of soccer. Who knows? By the end, you might just have a few wild facts of your own to share. Let's kick off!

Mind-Blowing Soccer Fact #1

MIND-BLOWING SOCCER FACT #1

THE GAME THAT LASTED THREE DAYS

The longest soccer match in history lasted **three full days** and shattered records for endurance!

In 1946, Stockport County and Doncaster Rovers played an **epic match** in the English Football League's Division Three North Cup that refused to end. After **203 minutes** of play—three hours beyond the usual 90 minutes—the game was finally abandoned due to darkness! Back then, stadiums didn't have floodlights, so the match simply couldn't continue. The teams had to replay the match, making this the longest officially recorded soccer game in history.

Mind-Blowing Soccer Fact #2

MIND-BLOWING SOCCER FACT #2

THE DAY A DOG WON MAN OF THE MATCH

A stray dog once interrupted a professional soccer match—then got named **Man of the Match!**

During a 2018 game in Argentina's **Primera División**, a playful pup sprinted onto the field and **stole the show.** The dog zoomed past players, dodged referees, and even stopped a dangerous attack by deflecting the ball! Instead of shooing it away, the players embraced the moment, and after the match, the dog was humorously awarded **Man of the Match** for its unexpected "defensive performance." The moment went viral, proving that sometimes, four legs are just as good as two on the pitch!

Mind-Blowing Soccer Fact #3

MIND-BLOWING SOCCER FACT #3

THE REFEREE WHO PULLED OUT A WHITE CARD

Soccer has red and yellow cards—but did you know there's also a **white card?**

In a historic moment in 2023, a referee in Portugal used a **white card** for the first time ever. Unlike red (for ejections) and yellow (for warnings), the white card is meant to **reward fair play** and sportsmanship. During a match between Benfica and Sporting CP's women's teams, the ref brandished the white card to recognize the medical teams **for helping an injured player.** Fans were stunned to see a new color on the field, proving that not all cards are bad news!

Mind-Blowing Soccer Fact #4

MIND-BLOWING SOCCER FACT #4

THE GAME THAT WAS PLAYED ON TWO CONTINENTS

One soccer match was played in **two different continents—at the same time!**

The **Sukru Saracoglu Stadium**, home of **Fenerbahçe** in Turkey, sits right on the border of **Europe and Asia.** Because of this, when a match is played there, one half of the field is technically in **Europe**, while the other half is in **Asia!** This makes Fenerbahçe's home games the only professional soccer matches in the world that are literally played on **two continents at once.**

Mind-Blowing Soccer Fact #5

MIND-BLOWING SOCCER FACT #5

THE MATCH THAT HAD NO BALL

A professional soccer game once started without the ball—because nobody noticed!

In a **2002 FA Cup** match between **Arsenal and Sheffield United**, the referee blew the whistle for kickoff, and the players began passing... **but there was no ball on the field!** For a few awkward seconds, both teams moved as if the game had begun, only for everyone—players, coaches, and thousands of fans—to realize the ball was missing! The referee laughed it off, the ball was finally placed on the pitch, and the game restarted properly.

Mind-Blowing Soccer Fact #6

MIND-BLOWING SOCCER FACT #6

THE GOALKEEPER WHO SCORED MORE GOALS THAN MOST STRIKERS

One goalkeeper scored **132 goals** in his career—more than many strikers!

Brazilian legend **Rogério Ceni** wasn't just an incredible shot-stopper—he was also a **deadly free-kick and penalty taker.** Over his 25-year career with São Paulo FC, Ceni smashed an unbelievable **132 goals**, making him the highest-scoring goalkeeper in soccer history. While most keepers stick to their box, Ceni proved that sometimes, the best way to save a game is by scoring the winner yourself!

Mind-Blowing Soccer Fact #7

MIND-BLOWING SOCCER FACT #7

THE WORLD CUP THAT WAS STOLEN

The FIFA World Cup trophy was **once stolen—and found by a dog!**

In **1966**, just before the World Cup in England, the **Jules Rimet Trophy** mysteriously **vanished from a display case in London.** The entire country went into panic mode, fearing it was lost forever. But just **seven days later, a heroic dog named Pickles** sniffed out the stolen trophy in a garden while on a walk with his owner. Pickles became an instant national hero, even attending the World Cup final as an honored guest!

Mind-Blowing Soccer Fact #8

MIND-BLOWING SOCCER FACT #8

THE PLAYER WHO GOT A RED CARD BEFORE THE GAME EVEN STARTED

A soccer player once received a **red card before kickoff**—even before stepping on the field!

In a **1998 English league match**, Plymouth Argyle's **goalkeeper, Jimmy Glass,** was sent off **before the game even began.** As the teams warmed up, Glass got into a heated argument with the referee over a minor issue. The referee had enough, pulled out a **red card**, and sent him off—before the match had even started! This made him one of the few players in history to be **ejected before touching the ball.**

Mind-Blowing Soccer Fact #9

MIND-BLOWING SOCCER FACT #9

THE MATCH THAT WAS DELAYED BY A SWARM OF BEES

A soccer game was once **stopped because of an unexpected invasion—by bees!**

During a **2018 match in South Africa**, chaos broke out when a massive **swarm of bees** stormed the field. Players, referees, and fans **ducked, dodged, and ran for cover** as thousands of bees took over the pitch. The game had to be delayed until officials could clear the buzzing intruders. It remains one of the strangest reasons a soccer match has ever been stopped!

Mind-Blowing Soccer Fact #10

MIND-BLOWING SOCCER FACT #10

THE FASTEST RED CARD IN HISTORY

A player was sent off **just two seconds** after coming onto the field!

In **2000**, English footballer **Lee Todd** set the record for the **fastest red card in soccer history**. The moment the referee blew the whistle to start the match, Todd muttered, **"That was loud!"** The referee took offense, deemed it **dissent**, and immediately gave him a **red card**. Todd didn't even get to touch the ball before being sent off—earning him one of the most ridiculous dismissals in soccer history!

Mind-Blowing Soccer Fact #11

MIND-BLOWING SOCCER FACT #11

THE GOAL THAT WAS SCORED IN JUST 2 SECONDS

The fastest goal in soccer history took just **2 seconds!**

In **2009**, Nawaf Al-Abed, playing for **Al-Hilal in Saudi Arabia**, scored an **unbelievable** goal straight from kickoff. As soon as the referee blew the whistle, Al-Abed **fired a rocket shot from midfield** that caught the goalkeeper off guard and landed in the net—**all in just two seconds!** This remains one of the **fastest officially recorded goals** in soccer history, proving that sometimes, you don't need to pass the ball to make history!

Mind-Blowing Soccer Fact #12

MIND-BLOWING SOCCER FACT #12

THE REFEREE WHO BOOKED HIMSELF

A referee once gave **himself** a yellow card during a match!

During an **amateur match in England in 1998**, referee **Graham Poll** accidentally **tripped over his own feet** and fell to the ground. Embarrassed, he jokingly pulled out his yellow card and held it up to **himself** for "simulation" (diving). The players and crowd erupted in laughter, making it one of the funniest moments in soccer history. While Poll later became one of the world's top referees, this remains one of his most legendary moments!

Mind-Blowing Soccer Fact #13

MIND-BLOWING SOCCER FACT #13

THE GAME THAT ENDED 149-0

The biggest scoreline in soccer history was a **149-0** victory!

In **2002**, Madagascar's **AS Adema** won a league match against **Stade Olympique de l'Emyrne** by an **insane** score of **149-0**. But here's the twist—the losing team **scored all 149 goals on purpose!** In protest against a controversial referee decision in a previous match, Stade Olympique players **deliberately kicked the ball into their own net over and over again.** The referee had no choice but to let the goals count, creating the most lopsided scoreline in soccer history!

Mind-Blowing Soccer Fact #14

MIND-BLOWING SOCCER FACT #14

THE FAN WHO GOT SIGNED AFTER ONE KICK

A fan once got **a professional contract** just for kicking the ball during halftime!

In **2013**, a fan named **Sam Bartlam** attended a match for his favorite club, **Al-Wasl FC** in the UAE. During halftime, he was randomly selected for a fan challenge and took a **spectacular long-range shot** that stunned the crowd. The team's coach was so impressed that he **offered him a trial on the spot!** Bartlam later joined the club's youth academy, proving that sometimes, a single kick can change your life!

Mind-Blowing Soccer Fact #15

MIND-BLOWING SOCCER FACT #15

THE PLAYER WHO WAS SOLD FOR 100 KILOGRAMS OF MEAT

A soccer player was once **traded for 100 kilograms of meat!**

In **1998**, an Argentine club, **Deportivo Rincon**, was struggling financially and couldn't afford to pay their players. Instead of cash, they **traded one of their midfielders, Adrian Bastia, for 100 kilograms of steak!** The unusual deal actually helped the club **feed the rest of the team**, making it one of the most bizarre transfers in soccer history.

Mind-Blowing Soccer Fact #16

MIND-BLOWING SOCCER FACT #16

THE SOCCER BALL THAT SAVED A MAN'S LIFE

A soccer ball once **saved a man from drowning in the ocean!**

In **2022**, a tourist swimming off the coast of Greece got caught in strong currents and was **swept out to sea.** Just when things looked dire, he spotted a **floating soccer ball** drifting toward him! Clinging to it for dear life, he managed to **stay afloat for 18 hours** until rescuers finally found him. Later, it was revealed that the ball had **floated away from a beach over 10 miles away**, proving that sometimes, a lucky bounce can be a lifesaver!

Mind-Blowing Soccer Fact #17

MIND-BLOWING SOCCER FACT #17

THE SOCCER TEAM THAT WAS BANNED FOR WINNING TOO MUCH

A team was once **banned from their league**—because they were **too good!**

In the 2012 **Madagascar Super League**, a team called **SOE** was so dominant that league officials **kicked them out** for making the competition unfair! Their unbeaten streak and massive goal differences made the league uncompetitive, so organizers ruled that they could no longer participate. Imagine being so good at soccer that you're not allowed to play anymore!

Mind-Blowing Soccer Fact #18

MIND-BLOWING SOCCER FACT #18

THE MATCH THAT WAS PLAYED WITHOUT A BALL

A professional soccer match was **played entirely without a ball—for charity!**

In **1986**, Dutch club **FC Haarlem** organized a bizarre game where players had to **pretend** they were playing soccer—but without an actual ball! Every pass, shot, and goal celebration was **completely imaginary**, with players and referees acting as if the ball was really there. The unusual event was held to raise money for charity, and incredibly, thousands of fans still showed up to watch!

Mind-Blowing Soccer Fact #19

MIND-BLOWING SOCCER FACT #19

THE GOAL THAT WAS SCORED BY THE WIND

A goalkeeper once conceded a goal **without anyone touching the ball—because of the wind!**

During a **2013 match in England,** goalkeeper **Sam Slocombe** took what seemed like a routine goal kick. But as soon as the ball soared into the air, a **powerful gust of wind** blew it straight back toward his own goal! The ball bounced once, flew over his head, and rolled into the net, leaving him and his teammates in complete shock. The referee had no choice but to **count the goal**, making it one of the strangest own goals in soccer history!

Mind-Blowing Soccer Fact #20

MIND-BLOWING SOCCER FACT #20

THE TIME A PLAYER BIT A CHUNK OFF ANOTHER PLAYER'S EAR

A soccer player once **bit off part of an opponent's ear—during a game!**

In **1994**, during a heated match in the German Bundesliga, **Bayern Munich's Oliver Kahn** lost his temper and **bit a chunk out of an opponent's ear!** The victim, **Heiko Herrlich**, was left in shock as Kahn had to be pulled away by teammates. The incident was so brutal that Kahn was given the nickname **"Der Titan"** (The Titan), cementing his reputation as one of soccer's most intimidating figures.

Mind-Blowing Soccer Fact #21

MIND-BLOWING SOCCER FACT #21

THE GAME THAT WAS PLAYED AT 16,000 FEET

A soccer match was once played **higher than Mount Everest's Base Camp!**

In **2022**, a group of professional and amateur players set a world record by playing a full soccer match at **16,000 feet (4,876 meters) above sea level** in the Himalayas! The extreme altitude made **breathing incredibly difficult**, but the players powered through, completing a **90-minute game on a glacier-covered field**. This remains the highest-altitude soccer match ever played—where even running for a few minutes felt like a full sprint!

Mind-Blowing Soccer Fact #22

MIND-BLOWING SOCCER FACT #22

THE TIME A GOALKEEPER SCORED FROM HIS OWN BOX

A goalkeeper once scored a goal **from his own penalty area!**

In **2013**, Stoke City's **Asmir Begović** made history when he launched a **goal kick** that traveled **over 100 yards (91 meters)** and bounced straight into the opposing net! The shot was so powerful—and caught the other keeper so off guard—that it set the **Guinness World Record for the longest goal in soccer history.** The most insane part? It only took **13 seconds** from when he kicked it to when it hit the back of the net!

Mind-Blowing Soccer Fact #23

MIND-BLOWING SOCCER FACT #23

THE MATCH THAT WAS PLAYED WITH ONLY 7 PLAYERS

A professional soccer team once had to **play an entire match with just 7 players!**

In **2021**, Brazilian club **Grêmio** was forced to take the field against **Internacional** despite having only **7 fit players** due to injuries and COVID-19 cases. Since FIFA rules state that a team must have at least **7 players to start a match**, they had no choice but to go ahead. Unsurprisingly, they were massively outnumbered and the match was **abandoned after just 6 minutes** when one of their players "suddenly" went down injured—leaving them with only 6 men and forcing the referee to call it off!

Mind-Blowing Soccer Fact #24

MIND-BLOWING SOCCER FACT #24

THE PLAYER WHO WORE FIVE DIFFERENT JERSEYS IN ONE MATCH

A player once had to **change his jersey five times in a single game!**

During a **2005 UEFA Champions League match**, AC Milan's **Gennaro Gattuso** found himself in a bizarre situation—his shirt kept getting **ripped, pulled, and torn** by opponents! By the time the match ended, he had worn **five different jerseys** because each one got **too damaged to continue playing in.** It remains one of the strangest wardrobe malfunctions in soccer history!

Mind-Blowing Soccer Fact #25

MIND-BLOWING SOCCER FACT #25

THE PLAYER WHO WAS SENT OFF THREE TIMES IN ONE GAME

A player once **received three red cards in the same match!**

In **2006**, English referee **Graham Poll** made one of the most infamous blunders in World Cup history. He showed **Croatian defender Josip Šimunić** three yellow cards before finally sending him off! Normally, a player is ejected after two yellow cards, but Poll **forgot to issue the red card** after the second booking. It wasn't until the third yellow that he realized his mistake and finally sent Šimunić off. This embarrassing moment effectively ended Poll's international refereeing career!

Mind-Blowing Soccer Fact #26

MIND-BLOWING SOCCER FACT #26

THE GOALKEEPER WHO WORE A CAP FOR SUPERSTITION

A legendary goalkeeper believed **his lucky cap** made him unbeatable!

Soviet Union legend **Lev Yashin**, widely regarded as one of the greatest goalkeepers of all time, was famous for wearing a **flat cap** during matches. But this wasn't just for style—he believed it **helped him see the ball better** and gave him an edge over opponents. Nicknamed **"The Black Spider"** for his incredible reflexes, Yashin remains the **only goalkeeper to ever win the Ballon d'Or**, proving that sometimes, superstition pays off!

Mind-Blowing Soccer Fact #27

MIND-BLOWING SOCCER FACT #27

THE REFEREE WHO BROUGHT A GUN ONTO THE FIELD

A referee once **pulled out a gun** during a soccer match!

In **2015**, a heated amateur match in Brazil took a shocking turn when the referee, upset over player protests, **went to the sidelines and returned with a loaded gun!** Players and fans **ran in terror** as he waved the weapon around, claiming he needed to "restore order." Fortunately, security intervened before anyone was harmed, and the referee was immediately arrested—making it one of the most outrageous officiating moments in soccer history!

Mind-Blowing Soccer Fact #28

MIND-BLOWING SOCCER FACT #28

THE WORLD CUP THAT WAS WON BY A COIN TOSS

A team once **won a World Cup match by flipping a coin!**

Before penalty shootouts were introduced, tied matches in international tournaments were sometimes decided **by a simple coin toss.** In the **1968 European Championship**, Italy and the Soviet Union played to a **0-0 draw** in the semifinals. Instead of extra time or penalties, the referee flipped a **silver coin** in the locker room—and Italy won! The Italians went on to win the entire tournament, making them the only team in history to win a major international title thanks to **pure luck.**

Mind-Blowing Soccer Fact #29

MIND-BLOWING SOCCER FACT #29

THE TIME A PLAYER DISGUISED HIMSELF AS A TEAMMATE

A player once **swapped jerseys with a teammate to avoid a red card!**

In a **1999 South American club match**, a player who had already received a yellow card **pulled off a sneaky trick** to stay in the game. Just before the referee could show him a second yellow, he **swapped jerseys** with a teammate and pretended to be someone else! The referee didn't notice at first, and the player stayed on the field for several more minutes before officials **finally realized the deception** and sent him off.

Mind-Blowing Soccer Fact #30

MIND-BLOWING SOCCER FACT #30

THE MATCH THAT WAS STOPPED BY A PARROT

A soccer game was once **stopped because of a talking parrot on the field!**

During a **2018 match in Brazil**, play had to be halted when a **parrot flew onto a player's shoulder** and refused to leave. Every time the player tried to move, the bird **clung on tighter** and even started squawking loudly! The referee had no choice but to **pause the game** until animal handlers arrived. The funniest part? The parrot kept repeating the same phrase over and over: **"Vai, Corinthians!"** — cheering for a team that wasn't even playing!

Mind-Blowing Soccer Fact #31

MIND-BLOWING SOCCER FACT #31

THE PLAYER WHO MISSED A GAME BECAUSE OF A VIDEO GAME

A professional soccer player once **missed a match because he was addicted to a video game!**

In **2018**, Arsenal's **Mesut Özil** was mysteriously left out of a big match. Fans speculated he was injured—until reports surfaced that he had been **playing Fortnite for over 5 hours a day!** Data showed that his gaming username had logged **more than 1,800 matches** in just a few months. Arsenal's coaching staff later suggested that his back problems might have been caused by **too much gaming**, making him one of the few players to miss a match due to esports addiction!

Mind-Blowing Soccer Fact #32

MIND-BLOWING SOCCER FACT #32

THE GOAL THAT WAS SCORED BY A TOILET PAPER ROLL

A roll of toilet paper once **accidentally helped score a goal!**

During a **2008 match in Argentina**, a goalkeeper went to clear the ball when a **toilet paper roll** thrown by fans blew onto the field. As he swung his leg, the paper **distracted him just enough** to mistime his kick. The ball barely moved, and an opposing striker **easily stole it and scored.** The referee allowed the goal to stand, making it one of the most ridiculous assists in soccer history—delivered by toilet paper!

Mind-Blowing Soccer Fact #33

MIND-BLOWING SOCCER FACT #33

THE PLAYER WHO BROUGHT HIS OWN PENALTY SPOT

A soccer player once **carried a piece of grass in his sock to take penalties!**

In **1986**, Argentinian striker **José Luis Chilavert** had a unique superstition—he believed he could only score penalties if he kicked from **his own perfect patch of grass.** So before every game, he would **cut a small square of grass** from his home training ground, **hide it in his sock**, and place it on the penalty spot before taking his shot. His strange ritual must have worked—he became one of the highest-scoring goalkeepers of all time!

Mind-Blowing Soccer Fact #34

MIND-BLOWING SOCCER FACT #34

THE TEAM THAT SCORED WITHOUT TOUCHING THE BALL

A soccer team once **scored a goal without ever touching the ball!**

During a **2013 match in Italy,** a goalkeeper from **Rimini** prepared to take a routine goal kick. As he stepped back to launch the ball upfield, his foot **got stuck in the grass,** causing him to **completely miss the ball!** To make matters worse, the ball **slowly rolled backward into his own net.** Since no other player had touched it, the goal stood—making it one of the strangest own goals ever scored!

Mind-Blowing Soccer Fact #35

MIND-BLOWING SOCCER FACT #35

THE TIME A TEAM WON A GAME WITH JUST ONE SHOT

A team once won a match **despite taking only one shot the entire game!**

During a **2018 Champions League match**, Greek club **AEK Athens** faced off against **Celtic** in a match where they were completely outplayed. Celtic **dominated possession, took 26 shots on goal,** and looked certain to win. But in a shocking twist, AEK Athens took just **one single shot the entire match—and it went in!** Their **100% shot accuracy** secured them an unlikely 1-0 victory, proving that in soccer, you only need one moment of magic!

Mind-Blowing Soccer Fact #36

MIND-BLOWING SOCCER FACT #36

THE COACH WHO GOT HIMSELF SENT OFF ON PURPOSE

A coach once **got a red card on purpose—just to watch the game from a better seat!**

During a **2016 match in Italy**, coach **Giovanni Stroppa** was frustrated with the referee's calls. Instead of arguing, he **intentionally stepped onto the field,** knowing it would get him **sent off to the stands.** His reason? He wanted a **better view of the game!** Fans later joked that he had upgraded himself to **VIP seating—without paying a dime!**

Mind-Blowing Soccer Fact #37

MIND-BLOWING SOCCER FACT #37

THE TIME A GOALKEEPER USED A WATER BOTTLE TO SAVE A PENALTY

A goalkeeper once **saved a crucial penalty using secret notes hidden in his water bottle!**

During the **2018 FIFA World Cup**, Denmark's goalkeeper **Kasper Schmeichel** faced a penalty against Croatia's **Luka Modrić** in extra time. But Schmeichel had a secret weapon—his **water bottle had notes taped to it, listing where each Croatian player liked to shoot!** Using this inside knowledge, he **dived the right way and saved the penalty.** Even though Denmark eventually lost in the shootout, Schmeichel's smart strategy made headlines worldwide!

Mind-Blowing Soccer Fact #38

MIND-BLOWING SOCCER FACT #38

THE MATCH THAT HAD 22 RED CARDS

A soccer match once ended with **every single player getting sent off!**

In **2011**, an Argentinian lower-division match between **Claypole and Victoriano Arenas** turned into **complete chaos.** A heated argument between two players quickly escalated into a **full-blown brawl** involving both teams, the substitutes, and even some coaches! The referee had seen enough—so he pulled out his red card and sent off **all 22 players.** This remains one of the most extreme mass ejections in soccer history!

Mind-Blowing Soccer Fact #39

MIND-BLOWING SOCCER FACT #39

GOAL DISALLOWED BY A FAN'S WHISTLE

A team once **had a goal ruled out because a fan blew a fake whistle!**

During a **2013 Spanish league match**, a player was through on goal and smashed the ball into the net—only for the referee to disallow it! The reason? A fan in the stands had **blown a whistle**, tricking the players into thinking the ref had stopped play. The referee was left with no choice but to **cancel the goal**, and the guilty fan was quickly **kicked out of the stadium.** Imagine losing a goal because of a prankster in the crowd!

Mind-Blowing Soccer Fact #40

MIND-BLOWING SOCCER FACT #40

THE PLAYER WHO SCORED A HAT-TRICK IN JUST 70 SECONDS

A player once scored **three goals in just 70 seconds!**

In **1964**, Scottish striker **Tommy Ross** set a world record by scoring the **fastest hat-trick in history** while playing for **Ross County**. His goals came in the **ninth, tenth, and eleventh minutes** of the game—meaning he completed his hat-trick in an **unbelievable 70 seconds!** The record still stands today, proving that sometimes, all it takes is one unstoppable minute to make history.

Mind-Blowing Soccer Fact #41

MIND-BLOWING SOCCER FACT #41

THE MATCH THAT WAS PLAYED IN THREE DIFFERENT DAYS

A soccer game once took place **across three different calendar days!**

In **2019,** a German lower-league match between **VfL Osnabrück and MSV Duisburg** began on a **Friday night** but had to be **stopped due to heavy rain.** The match was rescheduled and restarted on **Saturday,** but after just a few minutes, another storm **forced another postponement!** Finally, the game was completed on **Sunday,** making it one of the only professional matches to be played over **three separate days!**

Mind-Blowing Soccer Fact #42

MIND-BLOWING SOCCER FACT #42

THE TIME A GOALKEEPER WAS SENT OFF AFTER 10 SECONDS

A goalkeeper once **got a red card just 10 seconds into a match!**

In **2000**, English goalkeeper **Kevin Pressman** set an unwanted record while playing for **Sheffield Wednesday**. Just **10 seconds after kickoff,** an opposing player rushed toward him, and in a moment of panic, Pressman **handled the ball outside the penalty area.** The referee had no choice but to show him a **straight red card,** making it one of the fastest dismissals in soccer history—before he even touched the ball in play!

Mind-Blowing Soccer Fact #43

MIND-BLOWING SOCCER FACT #43

THE PLAYER WHO SCORED FIVE OWN GOALS IN ONE GAME

A defender once scored **five own goals in a single match!**

In **1994**, during a match in Madagascar's top league, defender **Radhouane Besbes** shocked everyone by **deliberately scoring five own goals.** Why? His team, **Stade Olympique de l'Emyrne**, was protesting a controversial referee decision from a previous match. Instead of competing, they decided to **own-goal their way to a 149-0 defeat!** This remains the most self-inflicted goals by a single player in one game—an unwanted record that still stands today!

Mind-Blowing Soccer Fact #44

MIND-BLOWING SOCCER FACT #44

THE TIME A GOAL WAS SCORED FROM A THROW-IN... ALMOST

A player once **scored directly from a throw-in**—but it didn't count!

During a **2012 match in Serbia**, a player launched a **massive throw-in** that somehow flew over everyone, **bounced once**, and landed in the net! The crowd erupted in celebration, but there was just one problem—**according to FIFA rules, a goal cannot be scored directly from a throw-in.** Since no one else touched the ball, the referee **had to disallow the goal.** Despite the bad luck, it remains one of the most incredible non-goals in soccer history!

Mind-Blowing Soccer Fact #45

MIND-BLOWING SOCCER FACT #45

THE PLAYER WHO BROUGHT A CHICKEN ONTO THE FIELD

A soccer player once **celebrated a goal by pulling a live chicken out of his shorts!**

During a **2009 match in Paraguay**, striker **José Pedrozo** stunned the crowd after scoring by **reaching into his shorts and pulling out a live chicken!** He had secretly **hidden the bird inside his uniform** before the game as part of a bizarre bet with a teammate. The referee was so shocked that he didn't even issue a yellow card—he was too busy laughing! It remains one of the strangest goal celebrations in soccer history.

Mind-Blowing Soccer Fact #46

MIND-BLOWING SOCCER FACT #46

THE MATCH THAT WAS STOPPED BECAUSE OF TOO MANY BALLOONS

A soccer game was once **delayed because the field was covered in balloons!**

During a **2008 match between Aston Villa and Sunderland in the English Premier League,** hundreds of **claret and blue balloons** (Villa's colors) were released by fans. The problem? The wind **blew them all onto the field,** making it impossible for the players to see or pass the ball! The referee had to **pause the game until stadium staff popped and cleared the balloons,** making it one of the most bizarre match stoppages ever.

Mind-Blowing Soccer Fact #47

MIND-BLOWING SOCCER FACT #47

THE PLAYER WHO WORE TWO DIFFERENT SHOES IN A MATCH

A soccer player once **played an entire game wearing two completely different shoes!**

During a **1995 Premier League match,** English defender **Chris Waddle** realized **just before kickoff** that he had forgotten one of his boots. With no time to get a replacement, he **borrowed one shoe from a teammate** and played the entire game with **two mismatched boots!** Despite the unusual footwear, he still put in a solid performance—proving that sometimes, skill matters more than style!

Mind-Blowing Soccer Fact #48

MIND-BLOWING SOCCER FACT #48

THE TIME A GOAL WAS SCORED AFTER JUST 2 TOUCHES

A team once **scored a goal with only two touches from kickoff!**

In a **2017 lower-league match in England**, a team pulled off one of the simplest yet most effective goals ever. The moment the referee blew the whistle, the first player **tapped the ball forward**, and his teammate **immediately smashed it from midfield**—sending it soaring over the goalkeeper and into the net! Just **2 touches and 3 seconds** after kickoff, they had already scored, proving that sometimes, less is more!

Mind-Blowing Soccer Fact #49

MIND-BLOWING SOCCER FACT #49

THE TEAM THAT FORGOT TO BRING THEIR JERSEYS

A professional soccer team once **had to borrow their opponent's jerseys—because they forgot their own!**

In **1978**, German club **Bayern Munich** arrived for a match against **VfL Bochum** only to realize they had **completely forgotten to pack their jerseys!** With no time to fix the mistake, Bayern had to **borrow Bochum's away kit** and play in their opponent's colors. Despite the mix-up, Bayern still won the match—though their fans probably had a hard time figuring out who to cheer for!

Mind-Blowing Soccer Fact #50

MIND-BLOWING SOCCER FACT #50

THE GAME THAT WAS PLAYED IN A PRISON

A professional soccer match was once **played inside a high-security prison!**

In **2005**, Brazilian club **Flamengo** was invited to play a **friendly match against inmates** inside the infamous **Bangu Prison.** The idea was to promote rehabilitation through sports, and shockingly, the **prisoners' team actually won!** Guards monitored the match closely, but the game ended peacefully, making it one of the most unique—and unexpected—venues for a soccer match in history.

Mind-Blowing Soccer Fact #51

MIND-BLOWING SOCCER FACT #51

THE TIME A GOALKEEPER PLAYED WITH A BROKEN ARM

A goalkeeper once **played an entire match with a broken arm—and still won!**

In **1935**, legendary Czech goalkeeper **František Plánička** suffered a **painful arm fracture** during a heated match. But instead of coming off, he **refused to leave the field** and continued playing with just **one fully functional arm!** Incredibly, he still managed to **make several crucial saves,** helping his team secure victory. His bravery cemented his reputation as one of the toughest goalkeepers in soccer history.

Mind-Blowing Soccer Fact #52

MIND-BLOWING SOCCER FACT #52

THE PLAYER WHO WAS SIGNED BECAUSE OF A VIDEO GAME

A soccer player once **got a professional contract because of his FIFA video game skills!**

In **2018**, English club **Burton Albion** made history by signing a player who had never played professional soccer—**but was a FIFA video game champion!** The club was so impressed by his **understanding of tactics and positioning** in the game that they invited him for a trial. To everyone's shock, he performed well enough to earn a short-term contract, proving that sometimes, virtual soccer skills can translate to the real pitch!

Mind-Blowing Soccer Fact #53

MIND-BLOWING SOCCER FACT #53

THE TIME A TEAM CELEBRATED TOO EARLY AND LOST

A soccer team once **started celebrating too soon—and ended up losing the match!**

During a **2013 match in Bolivia**, club **The Strongest** thought they had **won the game** after scoring in the final seconds. Players and fans erupted in celebration, and even their goalkeeper **ran to join the party** near the corner flag. But the opposing team, **Club Aurora,** quickly restarted play while the goal was empty and **scored from midfield!** The match ended in a draw, leaving The Strongest stunned and proving that in soccer, **it's never over until the final whistle blows!**

Mind-Blowing Soccer Fact #54

MIND-BLOWING SOCCER FACT #54

REFEREE USED ROCK, PAPER, SCISSORS TO DECIDE A MATCH

A referee once **used Rock, Paper, Scissors to settle a match decision!**

In **2018**, during an English women's league game, the referee **forgot to bring a coin** for the pre-match coin toss. Instead of delaying the game, he **asked the two team captains to play Rock, Paper, Scissors** to decide who would kick off! The moment was caught on camera, and while the captains laughed it off, the English Football Association **suspended the referee for not following official procedures.**

Mind-Blowing Soccer Fact #55

MIND-BLOWING SOCCER FACT #55

THE PLAYER WHO SCORED WHILE TYING HIS SHOELACES

A soccer player once **scored a goal while tying his shoelaces!**

During a **2012 match in Brazil**, forward **Luiz Adriano** bent down to fix his loose shoelaces **right in front of the goal.** Just as he was tying them, a defender attempted a clearance—but the ball deflected **off Adriano's leg and rolled into the net!** The stunned striker looked up, saw the ball in the goal, and celebrated one of the **laziest but luckiest goals ever scored!**

Mind-Blowing Soccer Fact #56

MIND-BLOWING SOCCER FACT #56

THE TIME A PLAYER GOT A RED CARD FOR KISSING THE REFEREE

A soccer player once **received a red card for kissing the referee!**

In a **2010 match in Spain**, Argentinian midfielder **Raúl Tamudo** disagreed with a referee's decision and decided to **protest in the most bizarre way possible—by giving the ref a kiss on the cheek!** The referee was not amused and immediately **showed Tamudo a red card for unsportsmanlike conduct.** The incident became one of the strangest ways a player has ever been sent off!

Mind-Blowing Soccer Fact #57

MIND-BLOWING SOCCER FACT #57

THE GAME THAT HAD THREE HALVES

A soccer match once **accidentally had three halves instead of two!**

In **2019**, a lower-division game in Mexico saw one of the strangest scheduling blunders in soccer history. After the **first 45 minutes**, the referee blew for halftime as usual. But in the **second half**, officials miscalculated the time and blew the final whistle **10 minutes too early.** After realizing the mistake, the teams were called back onto the field to play the remaining minutes—essentially creating a **third half!**

Mind-Blowing Soccer Fact #58

MIND-BLOWING SOCCER FACT #58

THE TIME A STREAKER SCORED A GOAL

A streaker once **ran onto the field and actually scored a goal!**

During a **1994 match in England**, a fan managed to **sprint onto the pitch completely naked** and shockingly **dribbled past the goalkeeper before tapping the ball into the net!** The referee, of course, didn't count the goal, and security quickly tackled the unexpected "striker." The bizarre moment left players and fans **in hysterics**, proving that sometimes, soccer delivers surprises no one can predict!

Mind-Blowing Soccer Fact #59

MIND-BLOWING SOCCER FACT #59

THE PLAYER WHO SCORED A GOAL WHILE LYING DOWN

A soccer player once **scored a goal while lying flat on the ground!**

During a **2014 match in Turkey**, striker **Ilhan Parlak** was tackled just outside the penalty area and fell to the ground. But as he landed, the ball **somehow rolled perfectly into his path.** Instead of getting up, he **swung his leg while lying down** and sent the ball curling past the goalkeeper into the net! It was one of the most unorthodox but incredible goals ever scored.

Mind-Blowing Soccer Fact #60

MIND-BLOWING SOCCER FACT #60

THE REFEREE WHO USED A SPRAY CAN TO DRAW A LINE

A referee once **brought a spray can onto the field to control free kicks**—and it changed soccer forever!

Before **2000**, players often cheated by **moving the ball forward** or creeping past the required 10-yard distance during free kicks. Brazilian referee **Heine Allemagne** came up with a genius idea—he used a **disappearing spray can** to mark the exact spot for the ball and the defensive wall. FIFA later adopted the idea, and today, this **magic spray** is used in almost every major soccer match worldwide!

Mind-Blowing Soccer Fact #61

MIND-BLOWING SOCCER FACT #61

THE MATCH THAT WAS PLAYED WITH A SQUARE BALL

A professional soccer game was once played using a **square-shaped ball!**

In **1962**, a Swedish league match experimented with a **new ball design**—a square-shaped ball, meant to improve dribbling and passing accuracy. However, the match quickly turned into **chaos**, as players struggled to predict the ball's unpredictable bounces. After just 30 minutes, the game had to be abandoned, and the square ball idea was permanently scrapped. Lesson learned: **some innovations just aren't meant for soccer!**

Mind-Blowing Soccer Fact #62

MIND-BLOWING SOCCER FACT #62

THE TIME A GOALKEEPER SCORED WITH HIS BACKSIDE

A goalkeeper once **scored a goal using his backside!**

During a **2011 match in Brazil**, goalkeeper **Rogério Ceni** attempted to clear the ball with a big kick. But as soon as he swung his leg, an opposing striker **blocked the shot—and the ball bounced off Ceni's backside, looped over his head, and into his own net!** It was one of the most humiliating and bizarre own goals ever seen, proving that sometimes, the ball has a mind of its own!

Mind-Blowing Soccer Fact #63

MIND-BLOWING SOCCER FACT #63

THE PLAYER WHO WAS SUBSTITUTED AFTER JUST 1 SECOND

A soccer player once **got substituted after playing for only one second!**

During a **2013 match in England**, midfielder **Keith Gillespie** was brought on as a substitute. As soon as the referee restarted play, **he elbowed an opponent in the face**—before even touching the ball! The referee **instantly showed him a red card,** meaning his time on the pitch lasted just **one second.** It remains one of the shortest appearances in soccer history!

Mind-Blowing Soccer Fact #64

MIND-BLOWING SOCCER FACT #64

THE SOCCER GAME THAT WAS PLAYED UNDERWATER

A full soccer match was once **played completely underwater!**

In **2019**, a group of extreme sports athletes in Austria organized the first-ever **underwater soccer match.** Players wore **diving gear** and had to **pass, dribble, and score while holding their breath!** The ball was specially designed to stay **suspended in the water,** and goals could only be scored by pushing the ball into underwater nets. The match lasted 30 minutes, making it one of the most bizarre versions of soccer ever played!

Mind-Blowing Soccer Fact #65

MIND-BLOWING SOCCER FACT #65

THE PLAYER WHO SCORED WHILE TAKING A DRINK

A soccer player once **scored a goal while drinking water on the sideline!**

During a **2018 match in Argentina**, striker **Carlos Tévez** walked over to the sideline to grab a quick sip of water. At that exact moment, his teammate intercepted a pass and sent the ball toward him. Still holding his water bottle, Tévez instinctively stuck out his foot, **deflecting the ball into the net!** The referee allowed the goal to stand, making it one of the most casual finishes in soccer history.

Mind-Blowing Soccer Fact #66

MIND-BLOWING SOCCER FACT #66

THE TIME A REFEREE GAVE A PENALTY KICK BY ACCIDENT

A referee once **awarded a penalty by mistake—because of a bird!**

During a **2015 match in Brazil**, a defender cleared the ball inside his own penalty box, but at the same moment, a **bird flew past the goal.** The referee **mistakenly thought the ball had hit the defender's hand** and immediately awarded a penalty kick! Despite protests from the players, the decision stood, and the opposing team scored from the spot—making it one of the most bizarre refereeing errors ever!

Mind-Blowing Soccer Fact #67

MIND-BLOWING SOCCER FACT #67

THE TEAM THAT WON A GAME WITHOUT TAKING A SINGLE SHOT

A soccer team once **won a match without taking a single shot on goal!**

In a **2019 match in Italy,** the team **Frosinone** faced **Sassuolo** in a tightly contested game. Sassuolo dominated possession and took multiple shots, but somehow **failed to score.** Then, in the **88th minute,** one of their defenders accidentally scored an **own goal!** Since Frosinone never took a shot of their own, they won **1-0 without ever kicking the ball toward the goal!**

Mind-Blowing Soccer Fact #68

MIND-BLOWING SOCCER FACT #68

THE GOALKEEPER WHO TOOK A NAP DURING A MATCH

A goalkeeper once **fell asleep during a game—because his team was too dominant!**

In **1954**, legendary Soviet Union goalkeeper **Lev Yashin** played in a match where his team was **so dominant** that the ball never came near him. With nothing to do, Yashin **leaned against the goalpost and accidentally dozed off!** When an opponent finally got a shot on goal, he had to wake up quickly and make a save—proving that even the best keepers can get a little too comfortable!

Mind-Blowing Soccer Fact #69

MIND-BLOWING SOCCER FACT #69

THE PLAYER WHO SCORED WITH HIS FACE

A soccer player once **scored a goal by accidentally smashing the ball off his own face!**

During a **2012 match in Spain**, striker **Álvaro Negredo** attempted a diving header, but the ball **bounced awkwardly off the ground and hit him square in the face.** The force of the impact sent the ball flying past the goalkeeper and into the net! Dazed but laughing, Negredo celebrated one of the most painful but unforgettable goals of his career.

Mind-Blowing Soccer Fact #70

MIND-BLOWING SOCCER FACT #70

THE GAME THAT WAS STOPPED BECAUSE OF TOO MUCH FOG

A soccer match once had to **be abandoned because players couldn't see each other!**

During a **1937 match at Stamford Bridge**, Chelsea faced off against Charlton in extreme fog. The visibility got so bad that Charlton's goalkeeper, **Sam Bartram,** stood in goal for **15 minutes** after the match had already been called off—**because he didn't realize the game was over!** His teammates had left the field, but he could barely see past the penalty box and just assumed the action was still happening. Officials eventually had to **walk over and tell him the game was over!**

Mind-Blowing Soccer Fact #71

MIND-BLOWING SOCCER FACT #71

THE PLAYER WHO GOT A YELLOW CARD FOR CELEBRATING TOO MUCH

A soccer player once **got a yellow card for celebrating his goal—before he even scored it!**

During a **2009 match in Italy**, striker **Mirko Vučinić** was through on goal with an open net. Instead of just tapping the ball in, he **took off his jersey mid-run to celebrate early.** But before he could kick the ball, the referee **blew the whistle and gave him a yellow card!** He was forced to put his shirt back on and finish the goal properly—making it one of the most premature celebrations ever!

Mind-Blowing Soccer Fact #72

MIND-BLOWING SOCCER FACT #72

THE PLAYER WHO BROUGHT HIS DOG ONTO THE FIELD

A soccer player once **ran onto the field carrying his pet dog!**

During a **2014 match in Argentina**, midfielder **Sebastián Pol** was celebrating his team's victory when he suddenly **ran onto the pitch holding his small dog!** It turned out that his pet had escaped from his home and somehow made its way to the stadium. Seeing the dog near the tunnel, Pol picked it up and **brought it onto the field for the post-game celebration!** Fans loved the moment, and the dog instantly became the team's unofficial mascot.

Mind-Blowing Soccer Fact #73

MIND-BLOWING SOCCER FACT #73

THE TIME A PLAYER GOT A RED CARD FOR WINKING

A soccer player once **received a red card just for winking at an opponent!**

During a **2016 match in Scotland**, midfielder **Dean Brett** was already on a yellow card when he got into a small argument with an opponent. Instead of saying anything, Brett **gave him a sarcastic wink.** The referee saw it as **unsportsmanlike behavior** and immediately pulled out a second yellow—sending him off! Brett later admitted he had no idea winking could get him ejected from a match.

Mind-Blowing Soccer Fact #74

MIND-BLOWING SOCCER FACT #74

THE TIME A FAN SNUCK ONTO THE FIELD AND PLAYED

A fan once **disguised himself as a player and actually played in a match!**

During a **1979 match in Brazil**, a die-hard supporter of **Grêmio** managed to **sneak into the team's locker room, steal a jersey, and walk onto the field.** Incredibly, the referee didn't notice, and he **played for nearly 5 minutes** before security realized he wasn't part of the squad! The funniest part? He even completed **two passes** before being escorted off the pitch.

Mind-Blowing Soccer Fact #75

MIND-BLOWING SOCCER FACT #75

THE GOALKEEPER WHO WORE THE NUMBER 10 JERSEY

A goalkeeper once **played an entire match wearing a striker's jersey!**

During a **1999 match in Argentina**, River Plate's goalkeeper **Germán Burgos** forgot to bring his kit. With no backup jersey available, he was forced to **wear the number 10 shirt—usually reserved for playmakers like Lionel Messi!** Despite the unusual number, Burgos still made several crucial saves, proving that **it's not the number on your back, but the skill in your gloves that matters!**

Mind-Blowing Soccer Fact #76

MIND-BLOWING SOCCER FACT #76

THE PLAYER WHO WORE A WIG DURING A MATCH

A soccer player once **wore a wig during a match to hide his hair transplant!**

In **2013**, French striker **Wesley Sneijder** had recently undergone a **hair transplant** and didn't want anyone to notice. To cover it up, he wore a **realistic-looking wig** during a game for Galatasaray. However, after a few minutes of running, sweat caused the wig to **slip out of place,** forcing him to remove it mid-match! The incident left fans laughing, and Sneijder embraced the moment with good humor.

Mind-Blowing Soccer Fact #77

MIND-BLOWING SOCCER FACT #77

THE MATCH THAT WAS DELAYED BECAUSE OF A SHEEP

A soccer game was once **delayed because a sheep refused to leave the field!**

During a **2016 lower-league match in Scotland**, players were warming up when a **sheep wandered onto the pitch** and refused to move. Every time someone tried to chase it away, it would **run back toward the center circle** as if it wanted to play! After several minutes of failed attempts, stadium staff finally managed to guide the sheep out—earning it a round of applause from the amused crowd.

Mind-Blowing Soccer Fact #78

MIND-BLOWING SOCCER FACT #78

THE GOALKEEPER WHO USED A TOWEL FOR GOOD LUCK

A goalkeeper once **refused to play without his lucky towel hanging in the goal!**

Legendary English goalkeeper **Bruce Grobbelaar** had a bizarre superstition—before every match, he would hang a **white towel** in the back of his goal. He believed it brought him luck and helped him make crucial saves. In one game, a referee **removed the towel**, and Grobbelaar became so distracted that he conceded two quick goals! After that, he made sure no one ever touched his lucky towel again.

Mind-Blowing Soccer Fact #79

MIND-BLOWING SOCCER FACT #79

THE TIME A TEAM WALKED OFF BECAUSE OF A BAD SMELL

A soccer team once **refused to continue playing because of a terrible smell!**

During a **2013 match in Bolivia**, the visiting team **San José** walked off the pitch mid-game, **complaining about an unbearable stench.** It turned out that the stadium's drainage system had **malfunctioned**, releasing a horrible sewage smell onto the field. Players were gagging, fans covered their noses, and after several minutes of protest, the match was officially **abandoned due to "unsuitable playing conditions!"**

Mind-Blowing Soccer Fact #80

MIND-BLOWING SOCCER FACT #80

THE TIME A DOG SAVED A GOAL

A stray dog once **ran onto the field and made a goal-line save!**

During a **2018 match in Argentina**, a team was about to concede a goal when, out of nowhere, a **dog sprinted across the goal line** and **blocked the ball with its body!** The goalkeeper was completely beaten, but thanks to the unexpected "defender," the ball stayed out. The crowd erupted in laughter, and the referee had to pause the game to escort the heroic pup off the field.

Mind-Blowing Soccer Fact #81

MIND-BLOWING SOCCER FACT #81

THE PLAYER WHO GOT A RED CARD FOR KICKING A BALLOON

A soccer player once **got sent off for kicking a balloon!**

During a **2011 match in Brazil**, a stray **red balloon** floated onto the pitch. Defender **Paulo Miranda** casually kicked it away—but the referee mistook it for **kicking the ball away in frustration** and immediately gave him a **second yellow card!** Despite protests, the decision stood, and Miranda became one of the few players in history to be sent off because of a balloon.

Mind-Blowing Soccer Fact #82

MIND-BLOWING SOCCER FACT #82

THE GAME THAT WAS PLAYED ON A FLOATING PITCH

A professional soccer match was once **played on a floating stadium!**

In **2012**, Singapore built a **massive floating soccer field** called **The Float @ Marina Bay.** The entire pitch was constructed on **a platform in the water,** making it one of the most unique stadiums in history. Players had to be extra careful—because if they kicked too hard, **the ball would go straight into the bay!** Despite the unusual setting, official matches and training sessions were held there for years.

Mind-Blowing Soccer Fact #83

MIND-BLOWING SOCCER FACT #83

THE TIME A FAN CONTROLLED THE STADIUM SPRINKLERS

A soccer match was once **disrupted because a fan hacked into the stadium's sprinklers!**

During a **2021 match in Spain**, just as the game was about to kick off, the **stadium sprinklers suddenly turned on, soaking the players!** Confused officials scrambled to turn them off, only to realize that a **tech-savvy fan had hacked into the system** remotely. The prank delayed the game for several minutes, and security was forced to **track down the culprit before play could resume!**

Mind-Blowing Soccer Fact #84

MIND-BLOWING SOCCER FACT #84

THE TIME A PLAYER GOT A YELLOW CARD FOR FARTING

A soccer player once **received a yellow card for farting during a match!**

In **2016**, Swedish footballer **Adam Lindin Ljungkvist** was already on a yellow card when the referee suddenly stopped the game. His crime? **Letting out a loud fart near an opponent.** The referee considered it **"unsportsmanlike behavior"** and gave him a **second yellow—sending him off!** Ljungkvist later claimed it was just **a natural reaction,** but the referee wasn't laughing!

Mind-Blowing Soccer Fact #85

MIND-BLOWING SOCCER FACT #85

THE GOAL THAT WAS DISALLOWED BECAUSE OF A FAN'S WHISTLE

A perfectly legal goal was once **canceled because a fan blew a fake whistle!**

During a **2002 match in Italy**, a striker broke free and scored a brilliant goal. But just before the ball hit the net, a fan in the stands **blew a whistle that sounded exactly like the referee's!** Thinking the play had stopped, the referee **disallowed the goal,** believing he had blown the whistle himself by accident. The furious team protested, but the goal never stood—making it one of the most frustrating pranks in soccer history!

Mind-Blowing Soccer Fact #86

MIND-BLOWING SOCCER FACT #86

THE TIME A REFEREE FORGOT HIS CARDS

A referee once **had to borrow a yellow card from a player—because he forgot his own!**

During a **2016 match in Portugal,** the referee went to book a player for a foul, only to realize **he had left his yellow and red cards in the locker room!** Embarrassed, he had no choice but to **ask one of the players to lend him a yellow card** so he could issue the booking. The moment left players and fans laughing, and the referee later admitted it was **his most embarrassing mistake on the job!**

Mind-Blowing Soccer Fact #87

THE PLAYER WHO GOT SENT OFF FOR CELEBRATING WITH THE FANS

A soccer player once **got a red card for hugging fans after scoring a goal!**

During a **2017 match in France**, striker **Issa Cissokho** scored a dramatic late winner. Overcome with excitement, he **jumped into the crowd** to celebrate with the fans. But when he returned to the field, the referee immediately **showed him a second yellow card** for leaving the pitch—**sending him off just seconds after scoring!** His team still won, but Cissokho had to watch the final moments from the locker room.

Mind-Blowing Soccer Fact #88

MIND-BLOWING SOCCER FACT #88

THE TIME A BALL BURST MID-AIR

A soccer ball once **exploded in mid-air during a match!**

During a **2014 game in Argentina**, a player struck the ball with so much power that it **burst into pieces mid-flight!** The force of the kick caused a defect in the ball's stitching to give way, leaving only **shreds of leather and rubber** flying toward the goal. The referee had to stop the game, and players couldn't believe what they had just witnessed. A replacement ball was brought in, but that shattered ball became an instant piece of soccer history!

Mind-Blowing Soccer Fact #89

MIND-BLOWING SOCCER FACT #89

THE PLAYER WHO CHANGED HIS NAME TO AVOID A CURSE

A soccer player once **legally changed his name because he believed he was cursed!**

In **2012**, Brazilian midfielder **Víctor Simões** was convinced that bad luck was ruining his career. After a series of injuries and poor performances, he believed his name was bringing him misfortune. To change his fate, he **legally changed his name to "Victor Bolt"**—inspired by the speed of Olympic sprinter Usain Bolt! After the name change, he claimed his luck improved, proving that some players will do anything to shake off bad vibes.

Mind-Blowing Soccer Fact #90

MIND-BLOWING SOCCER FACT #90

THE TIME A GOALKEEPER SCORED WITHOUT KICKING THE BALL

A goalkeeper once **scored a goal without even kicking the ball!**

During a **2013 match in England**, a goalkeeper made a routine save and **tossed the ball forward** to restart play. But as soon as he threw it, a strong gust of **wind blew it backward**, sending it sailing over his head and into his own net! The stunned goalkeeper could only watch as the referee awarded a goal to the opposing team, making it one of the weirdest own goals in soccer history.

Mind-Blowing Soccer Fact #91

MIND-BLOWING SOCCER FACT #91

THE PLAYER WHO BROUGHT A SELFIE STICK ONTO THE FIELD

A soccer player once **celebrated a goal by taking a selfie—on the field!**

During a **2015 match in Italy**, striker **Francesco Totti** scored a crucial goal and ran straight toward the crowd. But instead of a traditional celebration, he pulled out a **selfie stick hidden in his sock** and took a photo with the fans behind him! The moment became iconic, making him one of the first players ever to turn a goal celebration into a viral social media moment.

Mind-Blowing Soccer Fact #92

MIND-BLOWING SOCCER FACT #92

THE PLAYER WHO WAS SENT OFF FOR TACKLING A TEAMMATE

A soccer player once **received a red card for tackling his own teammate!**

During a **2011 match in Argentina**, defender **Carlos Arano** accidentally **slid in hard on his own teammate, knocking him to the ground.** The referee thought it was a reckless challenge on an opponent and immediately **showed him a red card!** Despite protests, the ref refused to change his mind, making it one of the strangest ejections in soccer history.

Mind-Blowing Soccer Fact #93

MIND-BLOWING SOCCER FACT #93

THE MATCH THAT WAS STOPPED BY A DRONE

A soccer game was once **stopped because of a flying drone!**

During a **2014 match between Serbia and Albania**, a **drone carrying a political flag** suddenly appeared over the field. Players and fans were confused as the drone hovered above them until an Albanian player **jumped up and grabbed it out of the air!** Chaos erupted as players from both teams started fighting, and the match had to be abandoned. It remains one of the strangest reasons a game has ever been stopped.

Mind-Blowing Soccer Fact #94

MIND-BLOWING SOCCER FACT #94

THE TIME A REFEREE USED A RED CARD ON A COACH'S CHAIR

A referee once **gave a red card to a chair!** During a **2019 match in Brazil**, a coach was so frustrated with a referee's decision that he **kicked a chair onto the field in anger.** The referee, instead of just warning him, **walked over and dramatically showed a red card—to the chair!** The crowd erupted in laughter, and even the coach couldn't help but smile at the bizarre moment.

Mind-Blowing Soccer Fact #95

MIND-BLOWING SOCCER FACT #95

THE PLAYER WHO GOT A YELLOW CARD FOR IMITATING THE REFEREE

A soccer player once **received a yellow card for pretending to be the referee!**

During a **2010 match in Spain**, midfielder **Sergio Ramos** tried to be funny by **mimicking the referee's gestures** after a foul. He pulled an imaginary yellow card out of his pocket and waved it at an opponent—**only for the real referee to immediately book him for unsporting behavior!** Ramos later laughed about the moment, but it was a lesson that referees don't like being impersonated!

Mind-Blowing Soccer Fact #96

THE MATCH THAT WAS STOPPED BECAUSE OF TOO MANY RED CARDS

A soccer game was once **abandoned because too many players were sent off!**

During a **1993 match in Paraguay**, tensions boiled over between **Sportivo Ameliano and General Caballero.** A mass brawl broke out, and the referee had no choice but to **send off a total of 20 players!** Since each team must have at least **7 players on the field** for the game to continue, the match was abandoned—one of the rarest ways a game has ever ended.

Mind-Blowing Soccer Fact #97

MIND-BLOWING SOCCER FACT #97

THE PLAYER WHO WAS SUBSTITUTED BEFORE KICKOFF

A soccer player once **got substituted before the match even started!**

During a **2017 match in England**, defender **Callum Elder** was included in the starting line-up but suddenly felt **ill during the pre-match warm-up.** Just minutes before kickoff, his coach decided to **replace him with a substitute—before he had even stepped onto the field!** This rare situation meant he officially started the game but never actually played a single second!

Mind-Blowing Soccer Fact #98

MIND-BLOWING SOCCER FACT #98

GOALKEEPER SCORED WITH HIS HEAD IN THE LAST SECOND

A goalkeeper once **scored a last-second equalizer with a diving header!**

During a **2001 match in the English Premier League,** Liverpool's **goalkeeper, Alisson Becker,** ran up for a corner kick in stoppage time. With his team trailing, he **launched himself into the air and smashed a perfect header into the net!** It was the first time in Liverpool's history that a goalkeeper had scored in a competitive match—and it saved the team from defeat in the final seconds!

Mind-Blowing Soccer Fact #99

MIND-BLOWING SOCCER FACT #99

THE PLAYER WHO SCORED A GOAL WHILE TYING HIS SHORTS

A soccer player once **scored a goal while fixing his shorts!**

During a **2015 match in Germany**, striker **Pierre-Michel Lasogga** was adjusting the drawstring on his shorts when a teammate unexpectedly crossed the ball into the box. With no time to react, he **stuck out his knee while still tying his shorts**—and the ball deflected off him and into the net! He barely even saw the goal happen, but it counted, making it one of the strangest finishes in soccer history.

Mind-Blowing Soccer Fact #100

MIND-BLOWING SOCCER FACT #100

THE GAME THAT LASTED ONLY 2 SECONDS

A soccer match once **ended after just 2 seconds** — the shortest game in history!

In **2004**, an English amateur match between **Cross Farm Park Celtic and Taunton East Reach Wanderers** was called off **immediately after kickoff.** Why? Celtic only had **seven players,** and as soon as the referee blew the whistle, one of them **pretended to be injured** so the game would be abandoned! Since a team must have at least 7 players to continue, the referee had no choice but to **blow the final whistle after just 2 seconds!**

CONCLUSION

Congratulations! You've just explored *100 Mind-Blowing Soccer Facts* and uncovered the **wildest, weirdest, and most unbelievable** moments in the history of the beautiful game. From bizarre red cards to unexpected goal-scorers, this collection has shown that soccer is much more than just a sport—it's a **global spectacle full of surprises.**

But here's the thing about soccer—it never stops evolving. For every fact you've read, there are **countless more waiting to happen.** Maybe this book has made you love the game even more, or perhaps it's opened your eyes to **how truly unpredictable soccer can be.** Whether you're a die-hard fan or just here for the crazy stories, one thing is clear: **soccer will always find a way to shock, entertain, and amaze.**

The beauty of this sport is that you never know what's coming next. Maybe the next **record-breaking moment** or **bizarre event** is happening right now on a field somewhere in the world. All it takes is a love for the game, a curious mind, and a willingness to ask, **"What's next?"**

So as you close this book, don't think of it as the final whistle. Think of it as **extra time**—because the game never really ends, and soccer's craziest moments are still being written.

Until next time, stay curious, stay adventurous, and remember: **the best soccer stories are the ones that haven't happened yet.**

ACKNOWLEDGEMENTS

Creating *100 Mind-Blowing Soccer Facts* has been a journey of passion, dedication, and plenty of last-minute deep dives into the craziest moments in soccer history. While my name may be on the cover, this book wouldn't have come to life without the inspiration, support, and contributions from some truly amazing people.

First, a huge thank you to all the **soccer fans, storytellers, and trivia lovers** who keep the game's wildest moments alive. Your passion for the sport and its **unpredictability** has been a constant source of inspiration. This book is a celebration of the bizarre, legendary, and mind-blowing moments that make soccer the most thrilling game on Earth.

To my family and friends—thank you for **putting up with my endless soccer stories** and for letting me go on and on about strange red cards, record-breaking goals, and games that had more drama than a championship final. Your support (and patience) means the world.

A special shoutout to **my readers**—you're the ones who make this journey worthwhile. Whether you picked up this book for the laughs, the jaw-dropping moments, or the perfect soccer trivia to impress your friends, **this book is for you.** Your curiosity and love for the game keep these stories alive.

And finally, to **the game of soccer itself**—thank you for being so **beautifully chaotic, endlessly surprising, and downright unbelievable.** You've given us moments that defy logic, rewrite history, and remind us why we fell in love with this sport in the first place.

Here's to soccer, to the stories yet to be told, and to the **craziest sport in the world.**

ABOUT THE AUTHOR

Felix Grayson is a storyteller at heart, driven by an insatiable curiosity for the strange, surprising, and downright **unbelievable** moments in sports. With a passion for uncovering the wildest and most mind-blowing tales from the world of **soccer**, Felix has crafted *100 Mind-Blowing Soccer Facts* to entertain, amaze, and spark wonder in fans of all ages.

When he's not digging through archives or chasing down the next quirky soccer moment, Felix enjoys **exploring legendary stadiums**, devouring sports biographies, and pondering life's most fascinating questions over a cold drink while watching the **beautiful game** unfold. A firm believer in **soccer's magic** and the power of a good story, Felix invites you on this journey through the sport's **craziest and most unpredictable moments**, proving that soccer is just as full of surprises off the pitch as it is on.

www.ingramcontent.com/pod-product-compliance
Lightning Source LLC
Chambersburg PA
CBHW030318080526
44584CB00012B/619